SandCastle 1

The Alphabet

Gg

Kelly Doudna

ABDO
Publishing Company

Published by SandCastle™, an imprint of ABDO Publishing Company, 4940 Viking Drive, Edina, Minnesota 55435.

Printed in the United States.

Cover and interior photo credits: Artville, Comstock, Corel, Digital Stock, Eyewire Images, PhotoDisc

Library of Congress Cataloging-in-Publication Data

Doudna, Kelly, 1963-
    Gg / Kelly Doudna.
      p. cm. -- (The alphabet)
    Includes index.
    ISBN 1-57765-400-5
      1. Readers (Primary) [1. Alphabet.] I. Title.

PE1119 .D6757 2000
428.1--dc21
    [[E]]   00-028886

The SandCastle concept, content, and reading method have been reviewed and approved by a national advisory board including literacy specialists, librarians, elementary school teachers, early childhood education professionals, and parents.

Let Us Know

After reading the book, SandCastle would like you to tell us your stories about reading. What is your favorite page? Was there something hard that you needed help with? Share the ups and downs of learning to read. We want to hear from you! To get posted on the Abdo Publishing Company Web site, send us email at:

sandcastle@abdopub.com

About SandCastle™

Nonfiction books for the beginning reader

- Basic concepts of phonics are incorporated with integrated language methods of reading instruction. Most words are short, and phrases, letter sounds, and word sounds are repeated.

- Readability is determined by the number of words in each sentence, the number of characters in each word, and word lists based on curriculum frameworks.

- Full-color photography reinforces word meanings and concepts.

- "Words I Can Read" list at the end of each book teaches basic elements of grammar, helps the reader recognize the words in the text, and builds vocabulary.

- Reading levels are indicated by the number of flags on the castle.

Look for more SandCastle books in these three reading levels:

Level 1 (one flag)	**Level 2** (two flags)	**Level 3** (three flags)
Grades Pre-K to K 5 or fewer words per page	**Grades K to 1** 5 to 10 words per page	**Grades 1 to 2** 10 to 15 words per page

Gabe grins for fun.

Gay gives Grandma
a hug.

Greta and Greg act goofy.

Grace and Gwen
giggle.

Gary pulls the wagon.

Gail helps in the garden.

CASH

Gloria has a piggy bank.

Gus holds his dog.

19

What does Grant feed?

(goat)

Words I Can Read

Nouns

A noun is a person, place, or thing

dog (DAWG) p. 19
fun (FUHN) p. 5
garden (GAR-duhn) p. 15
goat (GOHT) p. 21
hug (HUHG) p. 7
piggy bank (PIG-ee bangk) p. 17
wagon (WAG-uhn) p. 13

Proper Nouns

A proper noun is the name
of a person, place, or thing

Gabe (GABE) p. 5
Gail (GAYL) p. 15
Gary (GAIR-ee) p. 13
Gay (GAY) p. 7
Gloria (GLOR-ee-uh) p. 17

22

Grace (GRAYSS) p. 11
Grandma (GRAND-mah) p. 7
Grant (GRANT) p. 21
Greg (GREG) p. 9
Greta (GRET-uh) p. 9
Gus (GUHSS) p. 19
Gwen (GWEN) p. 11

Verbs

A verb is an action or being word

act (AKT) p. 9
does (DUZ) p. 21
feed (FEED) p. 21
giggle (GIG-uhl) p. 11
gives (GIVZ) p. 7
grins (GRINZ) p. 5
has (HAZ) p. 17
helps (HELPSS) p. 15
holds (HOHLDZ) p. 19
pulls (PULZ) p. 13

23

More Gg Words

ghost

glasses

gorilla

grasshopper